Leading The Storm:

How Calm Leaders Deliver Results under Pressure

Arben Gjokaj

ISBN: 979-8-234-01468-9

DEDICATION

This book is dedicated to my brother Ilir, for the
encouragement to keep striving.

If your actions inspire others to dream more, learn more, do more and become more, you are a leader.

John Quincy Adams, 6th United States President

CONTENTS

ACKNOWLEDGMENTS

To my wife and biggest supporter, Goca for editing and enhancements.

Walsh College President and Professor, Dr. Suzy Seigle for the feedback and guidance with the book.

Educator Ms. Suzana Boshnjakovsi, my 5th grade teacher who sparked the light in me for writing, all those years ago.

INTRODUCTION

Leading the Storm is based on the emphasis that leading others is a privilege. Therefore, leadership should be and is most effective when handled with care. This book is not just another leadership book; it serves as a guide for leaders who want to improve in order to lead more effectively under pressure, in a calm and composed manner. This method of leadership is not just beneficial for the leader, but maybe more importantly, for the team or organization being led.

The emotions and attitude of the leader set the tone for the rest of the team or organization, who are in most cases, the ones completing the tasks at hand and doing the work. If the leader is tense and on edge during escalations, the rest of the team is likely to respond in the same way. The quality of work and outcomes can then be expected to reflect that tone. I will go into more detail on the academic research regarding the emotion transfer phenomenon later in the book.

With a calm leadership style, not only does the quality of work improve, but the trust and confidence of the team also increase significantly. I do not know many people who trust someone who is known to yell or scream once things start getting tough. In those circumstances, people tend to keep their distance and work at arm's length. However, this is not helpful when escalations occur and immediate action is required.

It can be compared to a son or daughter who does

not confide in a parent about problems because mom or dad is known to overreact instead of lend a steady hand. Parenting is a form of leadership, just like any other leadership role in life. The concept of a calm, collected, and composed leader can be applied in any setting. Therefore, this book should also provide insight for anyone, in any walk of life, looking to improve their leadership style. I will outline nine principles to follow in order to take the required steps toward becoming a calm leader.

We all have something to learn from each other, and I will provide you with the knowledge I gained as a calm leader through my experiences and education. We are also all works in progress. Every day is a chance to improve ourselves through continuous learning, gaining insights from one another, and becoming the best versions of ourselves.

I believe we can only do this through a steady hand and a mindset that embraces a calm approach. We are then able to unlock our God-given potential and provide them in service to others in this world, as we are all meant to do. This is also demonstrated through examples of the great leaders in our lives and throughout history.

While some may have a calmer demeanor than others, becoming a calm and collected leader is a behavior that, like all behavior, is learned. It also does not look the same for everyone, based on different tendencies and personality types. However, calm leaders are composed under pressure because their leadership styles are built on solid foundations such as clarity, integrity, and structure.

The book provides examples based on my professional experiences primarily in the project management function. The 9 concepts presented in this book can be applied to any area of your professional career or personal life. Most objectives in life are done through project work, regardless of industry, professional, or personal title. You are likely part of a project team regardless of your specific role.

You might have picked up this book because you would like to be a calm leader but may think you are wired differently. I have news for you: we are able to change our thoughts and rewire our brains. There is extensive research proving that behaviors, and even aspects of personality, change over time.

This means we are all capable of reacting differently if our current methods are not working in our favor. By investing in this book and applying the knowledge offered, you can create new neural pathways in your brain to behave more calmly and composed under pressure.

This book should serve as your practical guide to become the admired leader in your organization or personal life. We are all capable of becoming better in our work and personal lives, continuing to evolve and grow with each passing day. I am also still learning to refine my approach every day and at times, catch myself slipping or reacting unconstructively. However, these instances serve as progress when recognized and adjustments are made accordingly. This process of learning eventually turns into wisdom. You cannot have wisdom without learned knowledge.

In the process of change we will stumble and make mistakes. This is a normal part of the process, just as any former smoker will tell you, it takes multiple attempts before you finally break a bad habit. The point is not to give up. With consistency over time (science suggests it takes about a month to form new habits), we can change our behaviors to better serve us.

Nevertheless, be prepared to go through the pains of growth as they are real. This is when you know real change is occurring, when you feel the discomfort through trial and error. This is part of the journey to success and refinement.

However, the pains of growth are not permanent. Over time, you will become desensitized, gain confidence, and with consistency, transformation will follow. I hope you enjoy this book and that it helps you get one step closer to developing to the amazing, God-given potential you are meant to become in this world.

PRINCIPLE 1: CLARITY BEFORE CONTROL

Organization creates freedom, not restriction.

Have you ever been in a hurry in the morning before work and attempted to drive your car with the windshield still icy or foggy? It is pretty hard to have good control of your car without a clear windshield. The odds of hitting something without seeing where you are going are reasonably high. The same argument applies when attempting to steer or control a team without clarity. Yet drivers and leaders alike attempt control before a sense of clarity all the time.

In my years as a project leader with an automotive tier supplier, I was once transitioned a major project that was suffering across all performance metrics. The poor customer relationship was likely due to the project being late on most deliverables, in poor financial health, and wrapped in confusion among the core team members. It was a mess! While the existing project manager was a likeable guy, he was highly disorganized in his approach to the project and the team, which made it almost impossible to deliver a product on good terms. The project had its complexities, which increased the need for solid handling.

I recall the countless escalation topics discussed in management meetings. These escalation topics often revealed missed deliverables due to confusion among team members, likely driven by unclear communication. The frustration among the core team members was evident during these meetings. Frankly, I was not even on the project and was tired of hearing about it. When the current project manager announced he was leaving the company, guess who the lucky guy was that had won the lottery as the new project leader? Me!

Before I officially took over and before the current project leader left, I conducted a thorough review of everything happening within the project. This is typically called a project handover phase, but most organizations have little to no formal template outlining how and what should be covered. I wanted to ensure I was clear on exactly what was happening in every aspect of the project, based on the amount of time I had to do so. The first step was to gain a thorough overview of all the components, how the components functioned, the open issues for each subcomponent, and most importantly, the status of the core team and overall stakeholders.

Without a clear picture of what was happening before attempting to take control, it would have been a messy start. I needed to understand as much as possible before taking the reins to limit the time spent figuring out where the messes were once we initiated cleanup. And as you may have guessed, I quickly realized that many open issues had ambiguity tied to them due to the poor handling of the project, which in itself was the core issue.

I did not rush in without first understanding the details I needed. Yet so many people call this a "sense of urgency", jumping into action without a clear understanding of the situation. I am sure there are examples of when that worked well, but I am willing to bet they are rare and a lot of luck was involved if it was successfully handled. You need to take the time to map out where the problem areas are before you can come up with solutions. This is where structure comes into play.

I am not saying we must wait until we understand every element before taking action. One of the cores of leadership is to make the hard decisions when things are unclear, which will be discussed in more detail under Principle 4. However, the point being made in this section is to understand the key elements as much as time allows before immediate action is required. As leaders, we develop this sense with experience.

The idea here is to organize the project in order to understand all the elements, at least to the best of your ability at the beginning. Extracting as much information as possible from the existing project manager was essential in understanding where things stood for each function. Sure, I could rely on and ask the core team members about the status, but only the project leader touches all aspects of the project and is responsible for the whole body. Core team functions are responsible for their specific lanes such as purchasing, quality, design, and manufacturing.

Once all the details were compiled and understood, I took immediate action to organize the project in a way that was clear for all stakeholders involved. It is not enough for the project leader alone to understand all the elements. The overall team should be clear on what is going on, at least from a higher-level perspective. This relates directly to the concept of clarity. When you have a clear understanding of the project status, this becomes the foundation for effective handling.

The first open issues meeting I held with the team consisted of a full project overview. The primary intention was to ensure that I understood all the issues at hand, but equally important was ensuring that the core functional leaders understood them as well. When projects are disorganized, communication usually suffers and tasks are often marked by confusion or missed entirely. Clarifying each open issue and ensuring it was captured correctly in the team's open issues list was essential as a first step before attempting to address them.

Once the issues were clear, identifying a single responsible owner with a clear execution plan was the next step. Avoid assigning more than one person to tasks, because then you open yourself up to finger pointing if something is missed later. As a team, we reviewed each open item and discussed what was required to execute effectively. One person was assigned to each task and owned it through completion, followed by an agreed completion date.

This is where communication becomes another key element. When I say communication, I do not mean just talking to someone. I mean fruitful discussions in an open setting that allow the team to feel comfortable enough to let their guards down in stressful environments. The team needs to reduce stress levels when communicating at the core team level. Only then is it possible to structure the team in a way that enables effective execution.

While a sense of urgency is at times necessary, it must be handled with a calm demeanor and clear, concise instructions. A sense of urgency does not mean adding stress to an already overstressed team. This approach is reckless, unhealthy in the long term, and will eventually demotivate teams.

This is not to say a leader should not display the type of sense of urgency that is *required* and many times expected from clients or customers. There are sometimes personality types or other leadership styles which may not easily align with this approach. I can recall at one time being accused of not portraying the *expected* sense of urgency by a particular high-demanding customer for an escalated issue at the time.

From that experience, I learned consistent communication was going to be required with the customer. I started by having a discussion with her directly to assure her the immediate steps were being taken to address the open issues at hand. In addition, I also emphasized based that on my experience, an effective sense of urgency should reflect order, trust, and clarity.

When you structure your work and tasks effectively, you immediately invoke a sense of calm within your team. A solid structure reduces unhealthy stress, increases motivation, and improves morale, acting as a jumpstart for performance. You are then ready to take on deliverables with confidence because you have a motivated and competent team to tackle the issues. This is tied to the second principle in the next chapter, where I will explain the role of emotional intelligence in sustaining performance under pressure.

A properly organized team and project make it far easier to manage all elements involved. When issues arise, you can quickly understand how to address them because you have the appropriate structure in place. How do you organize your project in this way? You do it by working with the team to ensure everyone has clear responsibilities within their respective functions and that every open issue has an agreed completion date.

With respect to organizing actual project elements, I have found that different tools can help. While some organizations offer Excel templates for open issues and PLM systems for documentation storage, items such as meeting minutes and other leadership responsibilities may require your own tracking systems. In the past, I have used OneNote from Microsoft Office for meeting minutes and for referencing key information. Today, there are AI tools on the market that organizations use to capture meeting minutes in real time, such as Wave and other similar applications.

Whatever method you use, the key is to find a system that works best for you to track the different elements of the project and the team. As a project or organizational leader, we are often required to multitask, jumping from one issue to another while holding everything together. This can be compared to a juggler in a circus act who showcases the skill of keeping everything moving without dropping a ball.

Occasionally, everyone drops the ball, especially before becoming proficient. This is part of the process with learning. It takes practice to become an effective juggler or organizational leader. With patience and determination, it is possible for anyone with the right attitude and mindset to develop into the calm and composed professional.

Once you build an organized structure within your team or organization, you will immediately feel a sense of control that may not have existed before. The reason is simple; you now have a clear windshield, or at least clearer. You will then have a better view of what lies ahead and the freedom to take appropriate action. You were only restricted when the project or team was disorganized.

Remember, organization creates freedom, not restriction. In Principle 9, I will revisit this concept in more detail as we explore organization and multitasking at a deeper level.

PRINCIPLE 1 Storm Readiness Checklist

Core Idea

Control follows clarity.

What This Looks Like

When things feel chaotic, the instinct is to push harder.

Urgency without structure creates more confusion.

Clarity reduces stress and structure restores control.

Apply It This Week

If you step into chaos during a storm (escalation):

1. List every open issue.
2. Assign one clear owner per item with agreed completion dates.
3. Establish a consistent team review cadence.

Self-Checklist

✓ Am I diagnosing the problem or just reacting?

✓ Is the ownership for each of the issues clear?

✓ Does the team feel calmer after I step in?

PRINCIPLE 2: CALM IS A LEADERSHIP SKILL

Emotional regulation is contagious.

Those in control are the calm ones. Have you ever experienced someone in a leadership role, whether in the workplace or in a personal setting, constantly yelling or shouting to get things done? It is usually a sign of a lack of control over the situation at hand. I like to think of it as a cry for help. Very few things today are worth yelling or screaming about, either in the workplace or in personal settings.

As a father of three children, I have had my fair share of experiments with yelling to get things under control. However, over time I have realized that it is not only unhealthy for me and my family, it is also ineffective for parenting. In addition, it is ineffective for any type of leadership in professional or personal settings.

I remember an experience with a difficult customer who was in a leadership role at a major automotive company during one of my previous jobs. While the customer's frustrations with our performance on a high priority project was warranted, I was unpleasantly surprised during a management meeting my manager invited me to attend. We walked into a conference room at the customer site to discuss our recovery plan for a major project I had just been assigned to in order to improve, which included high visibility at the customer and internal executive levels.

During our presentation of the root cause analysis for the issues at hand, the manager threw the handout we had provided across the table and began yelling, demanding that we present an immediate resolution plan. We calmly pointed out that the resolution slide was on the next page of the presentation he had just flung across the room. His frustration was rooted in the constant open issues we were experiencing at the time.

Nonetheless, I was in disbelief at the level of unprofessionalism I experienced in that moment. It was my first encounter with him. I could see that several of his colleagues were red in the face and visibly embarrassed.

The meeting ended as well as it could under the circumstances, though we did not complete our presentation. Follow up meetings were scheduled instead. I have not yet shared the real lesson from this experience. When my manager and I returned to our office and we had a chance to debrief, he mentioned that this particular customer constantly yelled. He described the encounter and his reaction to it using the old expression, *water off a duck's back.*

When my manager said this, I immediately realized that the customer's behavior was not only ineffective, but that our organization had become desensitized to it. It no longer had much impact, other than raising the customer's blood pressure. Not only was his method of dealing with a supplier partner ineffective, it also revealed that he did not have control over the situation. It was a valuable learning experience for me. I decided that unless I see a blazing comet heading toward us through the meeting room window, there is rarely a reason to react in the same manner.

When I reflect on that meeting, I believe we demonstrated professionalism by remaining calm and composed throughout the encounter. This was true even though we were technically in the hot seat as a supplier behind on a high priority project presenting a recovery plan. By maintaining composure, we showed the customers in the room that we were mature and professional, even in unstable situations where we could have easily reacted otherwise. Emotional stability restores focus and trust.

Staying calm in difficult situations does not come naturally for most of us. Even those who appear to have a calm demeanor have typically developed it over time. Like any skill, it requires practice to control your reactions in a way that differs from our default tendencies. It can be developed through deliberate effort and reflection. A good place to start is by practicing calm responses in your personal life.

Before deciding to return to college to complete my bachelor's degree in business, I was interested in becoming a firefighter. I will not go into the reasons for how I transitioned from that path to the corporate world, but the point is that previous experiences shape us, often in ways that benefit us later in life. In order to become a firefighter in much of suburban America, you are typically required to first become licensed as an emergency medical technician.

To pursue this career at the time, I obtained my license and worked for several years at a local private EMS ambulance service. While much of the work involved non-emergency transport, there were many times when we were called as emergency backup when municipal services were overwhelmed. Without going into specific examples, I saw my share of critical cases and emergencies.

One of the most important skills I developed was the ability to remain calm in urgent situations, while still acting with urgency. No situation warranted jumping in without first assessing the surroundings to ensure the scene was safe. This is the first principle taught in emergency care, protect yourself and analyze the situation before initiating care. Think about that. We are talking about training for life-or-death situations. Now compare this to our tendency to jump into situations in the office environment because we consider an issue to be top priority.

Another critical skill I developed in EMS was communication, especially with patients. You encounter people from all walks of life in highly emotional moments. People are not typically having a good day when they call EMS. They are often emotionally charged when you arrive. You learn quickly that calming the situation is part of delivering effective care.

When I later stepped into the corporate world, many of the escalations and stress filled situations seemed minor in comparison. I can recall my observations with watching people in dress shirts running around in visible panic, yet no one was dying or seriously hurt. If I had not had my EMS experience, I might have mirrored those high stress behaviors. Instead, I entered the corporate world with a different lens. For those who have read Stephen Covey's *7 Habits of Highly Effective People*, you understand how powerful perspective can be and how the lens through which you view the world shapes your perspective.

Staying calm is also a beneficial skill for your customer communication. There are times when I would receive phone calls from customers in panic mode over a quality or manufacturing issue which needed to be resolved right away. My calm tone and composed response also calmed the customer on the other end of the phone line. It wasn't just my tone which did it; I explained the immediate steps I would take to contain the situation. However, if I would have responded in a panic mode as well, it would not have helped calm the situation and cluttered by thinking. I would often receive emails or calls from customers after the fact, thanking me for keeping a professional composure and a steady hand in my communication.

I would argue that it is often easier to stay calm professionally than personally. The reason is simple. In your personal life, you feel freer to express yourself openly. In the workplace, most people follow a set of expected behaviors. Whether you work in the corporate world, the service industry, construction, or healthcare, a level of professionalism is required. Most people strive to maintain at least a minimum standard of behavior.

The opportunity is to exceed the minimum expectation by becoming the steady presence in the office, restaurant, hospital wing, or construction site. You do this by thinking before reacting and by not allowing emotions to dictate your behavior. With a few tips I will outline at the end of this chapter, you can start with my steps and tweak as necessary based on what works best for you.

We are all human and full of emotion. Emotions are natural. However, behavior is a choice. We have control over our actions, regardless of the emotions we feel in the moment. This is what academia refers to as emotional intelligence, often called EQ. Harvard Business School defines it as the ability to manage your own emotions and recognize and influence the emotions of those around you.

The evidence supporting strong emotional intelligence is compelling. Research consistently shows that EQ is one of the strongest predictors of performance in the workplace. For those who aspire to executive or senior leadership roles, strong emotional intelligence is no longer optional; it is expected. Whether you work in a corporation or run your own business, the research is clear about the type of behavior that drives effective leadership today.

Research indicates emotions are highly contagious at both the individual and group levels. This phenomenon is known as emotional contagion. Researchers describe people as walking mood inductors, meaning they continually influence the moods and judgments of those around them. The evidence is clear; emotions create ripple effects.

I'll give you an example of this phenomenon with one of my previous experiences. I became good friends with a colleague at work after many years in similar roles. We used to let off steam, or vent to each other about work related issues all the time, especially during lunch. However, he was constantly complaining about things. I would laugh more than anything because I found it interesting how much he loved complaining.

One day I received the news that he had put in his 2 weeks' notice of resignation. When I heard, I was not happy because he had become a good friend. After a few weeks of him leaving though, I noticed I felt lighter on my feet and more energized in my workplace. The negativity and constant complaints were draining me subconsciously and I wasn't even aware of it until he had left the company. I literally felt the weight releasing from my shoulders.

This is the first time I consciously realized the effects we have on each other. Before this occurred to me, I never gave it much thought. It never occurred to me the amount of positive or negative influence someone can have on you by being around them. This is important to note and to consider those around us to understand if they're helping or hurting us, even unknowingly.

Years later, I found he had changed his behavior and was no longer a constant complainer. Because of this, we are still friends today and we remain in contact. It is important to realize the impact others have on you. In my case, I didn't even realize the impact it was having on me mentally in my job until after the fact.

If you are spending time with someone who may be a drag on you, educate them to adjust their behavior so it better serves you *and them*. If that is not possible – limit your time with these individuals. And the inverse is true, keep the ones who motivate you and have a positive influence on you close and within your orbit.

So, what else can we do with this information? First, we acknowledge that we have control over our own behavior. There may be moments when tears or laughter come naturally, but in the workplace our composure is typically driven by intent. We are not watching soap operas or comedy shows during working hours, unless that is part of our job. Even then, repeated exposure builds emotional regulation.

Once we recognize that control is within our reach, we can adjust our behavior accordingly. One of the advantages of being human is the ability to pause and think before acting. We are not hardwired for automatic reactions. Unlike animals that respond instinctively to their environment, we have the ability to reflect and choose a measured response. In most workplace scenarios, we are not facing imminent danger. The emotional impulse can be contained long enough to make a better, more informed decision.

Why should we care about being calm if we are getting things done anyway? Because calmness produces better outcomes. It supports stronger decision making, more effective leadership, and greater satisfaction among team members. These factors contribute directly to improved performance and better business results.

This raises the next logical question: if calmness enhances performance and influence, how do we intentionally develop it as a leadership strength rather than leaving it to personality or chance...

Here are 3 easy steps to follow which you can adopt immediately. During a stressful event, when we notice the pressure building or the tightness in our chest, pause and acknowledge it in your head.

Realize this and avoid the urge to want to react emotionally right away. The next step is crucial: take a deep breath (or a few of them) and release some of the pressure with it.

Notice how I did not say ALL of the pressure. The reason for this is because some pressure is good for us as it motivates us to take action. However, too much pressure or stress is obviously unhealthy. Final step: ensure to keep your voice steady and tempered appropriately in your response. Your mindset will lead your behavior.

Friendly reminder: this will not come naturally to you in the beginning. However, over time and with consistency you will create new pathways in your brain and develop the skill to keep cool in any scenario, even in those situations when everyone else is seemingly running around with their heads on fire.

I will share a story about customer related pressures as it related to operational integrity in the next chapter under principle 3.

PRINCIPLE 2 Storm Readiness Checklist

Core Idea

Your emotional control sets the tone for everyone else.

What This Looks Like

When things go wrong, people don't look for the loudest voice; they look for the most stable one.

Calm doesn't mean passive. It means controlled.

Apply It This Week

When under pressure, follow these steps to stay calm:

1. Pause and notice the pressure build up.
2. Take a deep breath and release some of the pressure with it.
3. Lower your inner voice before responding.

Self-Checklist

- ✓ Am I stabilizing the room or adding to the stress?

- ✓ Am I remembering people's emotions are contagious?

- ✓ Am I allowing my emotions to dictate my behavior?

PRINCIPLE 3: INTEGRITY IS OPERATIONAL

Doing what you say you'll do—or communicating when you can't.

There is an old saying in project management, *under promise and over deliver*. This goes beyond integrity; it means committing only to what you know you can deliver and when possible, delivering before you said you would. It does not mean agreeing to something when you know you cannot achieve it or when you lack the confidence to determine how long it will realistically take.

Unfortunately, people tend to remember the one time you lied or failed to deliver more than the many times you told the truth. It is tempting to say yes or to promise a date when under pressure from a customer. I have been in those situations many times in my career where it felt easier to agree to a deliverable you likely will not meet than to say no. However, in my experience when you commit to a timeline that even the customer may suspect is unrealistic, you are the one held accountable when the date is missed. It is typically not the customer's fault when you miss the date even if they pressured you into agreeing to it.

This is where emotional intelligence and courage are required. When you know you are unlikely to meet a requested deadline it is best to be honest upfront, even if it means your customer is initially unhappy. It is better to face the tension at the beginning and work through it together than to promise an impossible deadline and lose trust in the process.

In project management where I have spent most of my professional career, on time delivery is one of the primary objectives of the role. As a result, I have been placed in many difficult situations with customers and internal stakeholders who have consistently challenged my timing plans and planned completion dates. There are many examples I could share, but one stands out in my mind in particular.

I often share experiences with tougher customers because those situations tend to offer the most valuable lessons. In one case, a customer repeatedly challenged the timing plan I had presented to him and his leadership team. I understood the pressure he was under from his superiors to resolve a high stakes quality issue affecting their vehicles.

While I was fully aware of the urgency, I was equally aware of the validation process required to implement a proper fix. We had already compressed the timeline wherever possible without affecting the quality. I knew there was no additional room for improvements.

I communicated this clearly, along with my usual statement at the time that we would improve timing wherever feasible as we progressed. I was on daily calls with the customer, and each call included another attempt by the customer to challenge our completion dates. It felt like it was never ending.

Every *single day* for months my response remained the same, "no, we cannot pull in any of the timing any further at this time." This became a recurring theme in each call. I remember explaining the process repeatedly, reviewing in detail why we could not bypass critical steps or speed up any of the required validation from the plan. At times, I would ask the customer if he preferred that I lie, because even then it would not change the reality that we could not commit to earlier completion dates.

This approach may appear rigid, but there are times when you must remain firm in the face of pressure. This is especially true when you know the facts and understand that the likelihood of achieving the requested outcome is low. Often, the customer is under pressure from their own leadership to push you for earlier dates. However, if you agree to an unrealistic target and fail to meet it, you will be the one in the hotseat. It takes practice, but over time you become more comfortable standing firm rather than making promises which lead to failure.

Providing reality upfront also helps prevent larger escalations later. It may trigger escalation earlier, but it is far better to address the issue immediately than to allow it to drag on and worsen over time. Many problems grow when they are not addressed directly. If an escalation is delayed or minimized, it often resurfaces at a higher level when you can no longer delay.

If your organization conducts proper lessons learned sessions, it will frequently become evident when an issue was known earlier but not addressed properly or worse, concealed. That is not the path we want to take. I will discuss taking immediate action in more detail under Principle 9.

Being upfront requires courage, especially when the message is difficult to deliver. However, it builds trust with your team, your customer, and all related stakeholders. It also prevents problems from escalating unnecessarily. Ignoring a known issue is similar to identifying a disease and choosing to delay treatment. The longer it goes untreated the more difficult it becomes to manage.

A transparency-based approach communicates professionalism and seriousness. More importantly, it demonstrates that you can be trusted to provide accurate information. In the beginning, you may face intense questioning and challenges to your execution plans. Over time, however, you will earn credibility. Eventually, customers will rely on your word, which makes future challenges easier to navigate. This is far more sustainable than being known as someone who repeatedly fails to meet commitments.

When you sign up for an overcommitment, you're signing up for overstress mentally for yourself and team. You will be pushing harder than necessary to complete tasks, which will in turn create quality issues down the road due to the lack of quality in the work. This is called cause and effect. The sweet spot is to allow your team enough time to execute in an *efficient* manner.

So, what is the key takeaway? Let integrity guide how you conduct business. Do what you say you will do and communicate clearly when circumstances prevent you from doing so. Be honest with yourself and with your stakeholders. The added benefit is this approach also simplifies your life significantly. I would rather not have to remember which version of the story I shared with someone, especially when managing multiple responsibilities at once.

Remember, when you tell the truth, it may create discomfort in the moment but it makes life easier in the long term. Information flows more freely among stakeholders and you avoid the risk of being exposed for an overcommitment. I have also found that while some customers may not appreciate the truth initially, once the initial uncomfortable silence passes, they often shift into problem solving mode and become partners in resolving the issue. This approach is far more effective than withholding information and attempting to resolve tough issues internally.

There are situations where immediate customer communication may not be necessary because the issue can be resolved internally and quickly. Even in those cases, honesty should remain the guiding principle. In the end, this keeps you and your team or organization on steady ground approaching challenges with calmness, consistency, and integrity.

PRINCIPLE 3 Storm Readiness Checklist

Core Idea

Integrity is execution aligned with your word.

What This Looks Like

Pressure creates temptation.

It is easier to promise what others want to hear than to defend what is realistic.

But credibility is not built by optimism.
It is built by accuracy.

Strong leaders commit only to what they can deliver.

Stand firm when pressured into unrealistic timelines.

Apply It This Week

1. Review one commitment you've made. Is it realistic?

2. If risk exists, communicate it now — not later.

3. When timelines shift, inform stakeholders before they ask.

Self-Check

- ✓ Do I overcommit under pressure?

- ✓ Do I delay difficult conversations?

- ✓ Would my team describe my timelines as reliable?

PRINCIPLE 4: EXECUTION IS A FORM OF RESPECT

People deserve leaders who move things forward.

There are times when we are unable to retrieve all the necessary information before having to make a decision. These are the tougher leadership calls because there is always a chance your decision will be the wrong one and you will have to face the consequences. This is reality. At times, we will not have the clearest windshield to guide our decision making.

However, we can still make the best possible decision based on the limited information available and on the probability of a favorable outcome when time does not allow for further clarity. Leadership is not about waiting for perfect clarity. It is about moving forward *responsibly* when clarity is incomplete.

I was working with another major automotive company leading an innovation group responsible for bringing new driver assist systems to the market. A team in charge of a specific engineering function was struggling to reach consensus on their working approach for releasing software tied to their deliverables. Their method of work was too fluid to be effectively tracked in a standard open issues matrix. As a result, a different tracking method was required.

The issue itself was clear, but the disagreement among team members stalled progress. When I looked deeper, I realized the root of the conflict was discomfort. Some team members were uneasy with reporting methods they were not familiar with. A new type of agile system had been proposed, which introduced new tools and progression trackers. For several of the more traditional software developers, this created anxiety. They were comfortable with established company tools and standard style processes. Change, especially in technical environments often feels like too much risk.

I was also unfamiliar with the proposed agile processes. However, I recognized the type of innovative technology being developed required a more adaptive framework. The group was working on projects which were being released to consumer market for the first time. These were not incremental improvements. They required iterative development, flexibility, and rapid feedback loops. Traditional project management tools were not well suited for the way the method of work involved.

The team was stuck primarily due to resistance from a few of the influential engineers who strongly advocated for sticking with the existing company methods. Moments like this require leadership. As the project leader responsible for forward momentum, I first scheduled a one-on-one session with the team members who had the most experience with the new proposed agile system. I asked them to walk me through the framework in detail.

During the session, I quickly recognized the new system was not simply a tracking tool. It represented a different philosophy of work. It emphasized transparency, iteration, accountability within sprints, and continuous improvement. It aligned better with the innovation cycles we were navigating. While it would require me to adjust my own approach as well, I understood that the long-term efficiency gains outweighed the short-term discomfort.

Execution is a form of respect. Teams feel it when they are stuck in gridlock. Engineers, analysts, and developers want to build, solve, and create instead of debating process indefinitely. By taking the time to understand the issue and then making a decision, I was respecting their time, their expertise, and the organization's objectives.

Before announcing the decision, I sat down individually with the team members who opposed the new system. I explained what I had learned and addressed their concerns directly. I wanted them to feel heard. It was important they understood the reasoning, not just the outcome.

I did not want to impose the decision publicly in a way that would create resentment or embarrassment. The conversations were not perfect and the resistance did not disappear overnight. However, leadership required a decision and the decision was to move forward with the agile system and new tools.

Had I delayed further, the project would have slipped, problems would have compounded, and the eventual transition would have been even more painful because we would have lost valuable time. I did not conduct any complex calculations to measure the probability of success, but I knew the likelihood of improved execution with the new system was high. The cost of indecision was greater than the risk of moving forward.

The early stages were difficult. There were learning curves, misunderstandings, and inefficiencies. Productivity also dipped at time, especially in the early stages as the team adapted. However, this was normal as change always introduces friction at the beginning.

Over time however, the team became more comfortable. Execution improved and efficiency increased. Even those who initially resisted began to acknowledge the new approach made their work clearer and more structured. What once felt threatening eventually became empowering.

By making a decision as the project leader, I removed the uncertainty. The decision to move forward in itself was a form of respect. Time is a limited resource, especially in corporate environments tied to milestone commitments and market launches. Every day spent in indecision is a day not spent executing. When leading highly skilled professionals, it is our responsibility to create conditions where they can focus on delivering value rather than being stuck in gridlock.

I have always believed the hardest part of most things is the beginning. It is similar to an airplane preparing for takeoff; the climb to cruising altitude requires the most energy. Once at cruising altitude, the captain turns off the seatbelt sign in the cabin and forward progress becomes steadier and more predictable. This does not mean turbulence will not occur but the foundation has been established. Decisive leadership helps teams reach the desired altitude faster.

Indecision is a drag on efficiency and can become costly over time. However, decisive does not mean reckless. Hard decisions require thoughtful analysis and leaders must gather input, assess risk, and consider all implications. The key is calibrating the time spent analyzing against the urgency of the situation. In our case, we were operating under committed milestone dates. The cost of continuing debate of which method to utilize was eroding the time we needed to execute.

The ability to make decisive decisions comes

with time and develops with experience. It requires confidence, humility, and a willingness to accept responsibility if the outcome is not ideal. The most effective path is making the best possible decision with the information available and then committing fully to the execution.

Leaders are responsible for the team's momentum at the end of the day. Those being led deserve clarity, direction, and progress. Our role is to remove barriers and ensure the team has what it needs to move forward. It is not to add to the roadblocks or barriers by engaging in unproductive discussions or debates which are taking up too much time.

The subtitle of this chapter is *people deserve leaders who move things forward*. This is not an abstract concept but rather a practical expectation from those being led. Teams invest their time, energy, and expertise into their work. They deserve leaders who respect this investment by making decisions which enable progress.

However, moving things forward is not about

control. It is about honoring the responsibility that comes with leadership by ensuring your team can get to work. Once a team experiences the impacts of clear direction and consistent execution, they begin to trust you with your decision-making abilities. This is where the real gains are realized and you start to develop as a reputable leader. The earned trust then becomes the foundation for the next challenges ahead, and over time your decisions are fully supported by your team or organization.

PRINCIPLE 4 Storm Readiness Checklist

Core Idea

Forward movement honors the people doing the work.

What This Looks Like

Teams stall when leaders hesitate.

Debate has value. Analysis has value.
But prolonged indecision drains momentum.

When information is incomplete, leaders gather what matters most, weigh probability, and make the call.

Once the call is made, leaders own the outcome.

Apply It This Week

1. Identify one stalled decision.

2. Clarify what information is still missing.

3. Decide whether that information is essential or just comforting and make the decision.

Self-Check

- ✓ Am I waiting for certainty that will never come?

- ✓ Is delay protecting quality or protecting my comfort?

- ✓ Does my team feel movement or hesitation?

PRINCIPLE 5: MENTORING WHILE EXECUTING

Leadership is not pausing the work—it's developing people through the work.

I have many fond memories of mentoring others. I also have many meaningful memories of being mentored myself. There was a piece of advice I often gave to junior team members or new project leaders when they were stepping into a new role for the first time: *just jump in and you will learn*. What I meant by that is simple: growth does not come from standing on the sidelines.

The fastest and most effective way to develop is to begin, work through the kinks, and adjust in real time. This is how you ramp up without stopping the ship. This was also based on my personal experience.

Of course, the right attitude is required. If someone is not motivated to do well, no amount of exposure or opportunity will turn them into the kind of leader people look forward to working with. The leaders who are most sought after bring order, clarity, and trust. They are steady, reliable, and create environments where others can succeed. Becoming that type of leader starts with understanding that development happens through responsibility and not just by observation.

If you want to grow your people, give them meaningful responsibility and observe how they respond. Delegate important tasks and guide them along the way. Allow them to make mistakes when the risk is manageable and the lesson is valuable. That is how people develop. Mentorship is not about protecting someone from every failure. It is about walking beside them while they learn how to navigate challenges themselves.

For this to work, however, the leader must have a steady hand. When mistakes happen, and they will, they must be treated as learning opportunities rather than personal failures. If a mentor reacts with frustration or control, development shuts down. If the mentor remains calm and constructive, growth accelerates.

While leading a major program that included multiple subprojects, I was responsible for several junior project managers and their respective core teams. One of the project managers was new to both the organization and the role. The structure of the overall program created an ideal opportunity for mentorship while executing. I was accountable for the portfolio and directly overseeing his work, which allowed me to support him without removing ownership from him.

We made it clear to the core team members that this would be his first time leading a project team. That transparency mattered because it set expectations early and encouraged the right level of support from the team. A project leader can only be as effective as the team supporting them. When a core team commits to backing a new leader, that leader flourishes. Without team support, the road becomes unnecessarily difficult or even impossible.

This dependency highlights something important. Leadership is not a solo performance. Trust, integrity, and open communication form the foundation of strong team dynamics. These elements do not appear automatically but are built intentionally through consistent behavior. A leader who communicates openly and creates a comfortable working environment sets the conditions for a team to engage fully. Without this sort of foundation, both the project and its stakeholders suffer.

Once the team was aligned and supportive, we launched the subproject. Although I was responsible for the broader program, I paid particular attention to the subproject led by the junior manager. My role was to support him without overshadowing him. There were phases where the project hit rough patches with difficult customer calls and uncomfortable conversations. In each of those situations, I insisted that he take the lead.

I sat in the meetings for support and only stepped in only when questions fell outside his scope or required escalation. But from start to finish, he owned the communication, the decisions, and the accountability. There were no moments where I said, "let me handle this for you." The best way to learn the role is to live it, with calm guidance from someone more experienced.

There were late nights and stressful milestone but it was part of real project work. However, he was never alone. Development through experience does not mean abandonment, but rather it means supported exposure. Over time, his confidence grew as he navigated the project elements more effectively. Ultimately, he delivered on his milestones, closed the project successfully, and achieved healthy margins. The success was his and the growth was earned.

One important detail is that we never paused the project to conduct mentorship. The work continued throughout the project phases. If he did not understand how to run a technical review or complete a customer template, we worked through it during the actual meeting. Questions were addressed in real time. Development was embedded in execution, not separated from it.

A common issue I have observed among project and organizational leaders is the tendency to get stuck in the weeds. Details matter, but not all details belong to the leader. Sometimes we immerse ourselves in technical specifics that should be owned by the appropriate functional expert. If there is a mechanical engineer on the team, resolving a mechanical specification issue is their responsibility, not the project leader's.

Providing guidance or perspective is appropriate. However, taking over an issue clearly defined as someone else's function is not. When leaders become overly involved in technical details, they dilute their effectiveness. They begin working twelve hour days not because the workload is impossible, but because they are carrying responsibilities that should be distributed. Teams are structured with different functional experts for a reason. Each role has its own *swim lane.*

As leaders, our responsibility is to steer the ship and keep our focus on the horizon. We ensure alignment, remove barriers, and protect the bigger picture. When we micromanage, we signal a lack of trust but when we delegate appropriately, we demonstrate confidence in our team.

I once worked closely with a highly experienced and respected project leader at a previous Tier 1 automotive company. He was knowledgeable and committed. He also consistently worked twelve hour days. We used to joke with him about turning off the office lights before leaving or asking him where he hid his inflatable mattress. Over time, he shared that the overtime was creating strain in his marriage. Sadly, it was not surprising to any of us.

He was deeply involved in every open issue, down to the smallest technical detail. He enjoyed solving those problems, and his expertise was undeniable. However, by immersing himself in every layer of work, he limited his effectiveness as a leader. It showed in the projects he managed as he was not outperforming other project leaders in results. In executive reviews, his projects often showed the most issues. Meanwhile, other leaders including myself, were leaving the office at reasonable hours and achieving comparable or stronger outcomes.

The difference was the focus. When leaders operate at the right altitude, they see patterns, risks, and priorities more clearly. When they descend into every detail they lose strategic perspective. Respecting your team means allowing them to perform their roles fully. It also means respecting your own role and the boundaries that come with it.

On the job mentoring is how I learned best and it is how I have seen others grow most effectively. However, I could not have developed without the support of the teams around me. A leader without a supportive team is like an airplane without engines. It may look complete from the outside but it will never leave the ground. Teams provide the thrust while leaders provide direction and together, they move forward.

Developing people through real responsibility is not only efficient but it is respectful because it communicates belief in their potential.

As a result, when people feel trusted and supported they rise to the level expected of them.

PRINCIPLE 5 Storm Readiness Checklist

Core Idea

Development happens in motion, not on pause.

What This Looks Like

Let people lead while you stay close enough to support, but far enough not to interfere.

If you always take over, they never grow. You then also won't grow as an effective leader.

Don't micromanage - give your people the runway needed to take off!

Apply It This Week

1. If someone can do the task or wants to take ownership, delegate it.
2. Stay available in case they need you.
3. Do not take the task back unless absolutely necessary.

Self-Checklist

- ✓ Am I leading or doing?

- ✓ Am I developing or controlling?

- ✓ Am I sufficiently focused on the direction or focused too much on the details?

PRINCIPLE 6: INFLUENCE WITHOUT AUTHORITY

Credibility outlasts position.

The majority of my career as a project leader consisted of having no direct supervision over the project teams. Most corporations structure project teams this way, with functional teams reporting to their respective functional managers or directors. Matrix organizations typically follow this format for their organizational structures.

The project manager or leader manages the

project and indirectly manages the team from a supervision standpoint. I have also had the privilege of directly supervising junior project leaders. In both cases, credibility proved to be a key influence with the team or organization while position or authority did not carry the same lasting impact.

In the beginning of most projects I have managed, especially high priority ones, I started the initial team meetings by ensuring everyone understood the trust instilled in us by the organization and the rewarding experience we should anticipate with successful execution. I explained to the team members that each of us had been given the opportunity to deliver a remarkable product to market based on our expertise and knowledge. We were credible enough for the organization to trust us with that responsibility.

Credibility is established through consistency and by example. I have heard similar statements about respect, with the common saying that respect must be earned. I reject that notion. Respect is expected in human interaction, regardless of whether you know the person or not. You should hold the door for someone entering a store behind you just as you would address someone you do not know as sir or ma'am. Both are forms of respect for another human being. However, while respect is expected, it can be lost when expectations are not met.

Credibility, on the other hand, is not assumed from the outset. It must be earned. Showing up for your team consistently and being present when they require leadership, motivation, and support to overcome roadblocks is how credibility is built. People quickly sense when someone does not genuinely care or is halfhearted in their commitment. As a leader, the key is to provide authentic support from a positive mindset and a stable emotional state.

I cannot count the number of times I have gone out of my way for team members, nor the number of times they have gone the extra mile for me. That is what project success looks like and how credibility is built within a team. It is established by committing to support one another and delivering on objectives together. Over time, you earn the reputation of being a dependable and stable leader whom the organization can rely on without hesitation.

Once credibility is earned, the potential for advancement within the organization increases significantly. As trust is built with your teams, you become recognized as a source of competence and leadership capability. Opportunities for more challenging and exciting leadership roles begin to emerge, and you gain the ability to shape your own direction. This occurs because you have unlocked credibility within the organization.

After delivering several high priority projects to successful completion and closure, I was provided with advancement opportunities and increased earning potential. Organizations recognize credible leaders who execute effectively, and retaining individuals of that caliber aligns with their best interests. This is why maintaining a calm mindset and patience is important. Progress takes time. You must first prove to yourself, and then to others, that you are capable.

The recognition and advancement I

experienced over the years would not have been possible without the teams supporting my growth and objectives. Their motivation and consistent performance propelled me to higher levels of responsibility. As mentioned beforehand, as a leader you are only as good as your team. The simple fact is no one can achieve great things alone.

Think of the pirate movies or any with a ship crew. The captain gives the commands and the crew immediately get to work. Some climb the mast to release the sails, others release the anchor, etc. The principle is simple; you delegate, trust your team, and hold them accountable. If something is delayed or obstacles arise, it is your responsibility as the leader to help remove those barriers so progress can continue.

Over time, you become more proficient at supporting your team and your credibility grows. Trust is earned through repeated experiences of stable, supportive, and effective leadership. There will be times when objectives are missed. Those moments should be communicated clearly to the team as lessons learned and opportunities to improve future execution.

Credibility is earned through time with trial-and-error periods. There will be times when execution does not match with your intended objectives or you just don't meet them. During those times, you must remain as a source of steady guidance by treating the wrong decisions for what they really are — lessons learned.

The same goes for team members when you delegate and they experience a missed deliverable. You also build trust by delegating meaningful tasks and empowering others to contribute to the main objectives. You talk about it as a team, adjust as needed, and try again. This type of leadership strengthens your credibility.

While authority is common in leadership roles, it is not always necessary to drive performance. Credibility will outlast authority in the long run. Strong leadership attracts high performing teams whereas authority alone is fixed and limited. A poor manager may compel compliance, but cannot inspire people to give their best effort.

Authority has limitations, especially when leadership is ineffective. In many workplaces, authority is reinforced primarily by compensation since people need income to live. However, with credibility, influence increases because people trust the competence and guidance of their leader. Compensation may motivate short term effort, but over time people adapt to their financial situation and seek more meaningful engagement from their work.

I have experienced authority without credibility firsthand. I previously worked for a micromanager who required visibility into every issue at all times. While this was occasionally helpful during executive level escalations, it often created unnecessary work for me and the teams. The organization became a revolving door, with employees leaving within six months to a year. Escalations were constant.

In retrospect, the missing element was credibility. Although the manager was a good person personally, he lacked credibility within the organization because he was unwilling to delegate effectively or allow team members to take ownership of issues. Once a task was assigned, he demanded constant follow ups, which prevented the team from focusing on solving the problem and instead redirected their energy toward preparing status updates.

You cannot build credibility without demonstrating trust in your team. If you hold authority but cannot seem to trust your team, why did you hire them? Without trust, the team cannot gain momentum.

It would be like a pilot leaving the cockpit before takeoff to personally check whether the cabin crew ensured passengers were buckled in, tray tables were up, and seats were upright. It makes no sense and defeats the purpose of having a crew. You hire capable people so you can focus on your responsibilities. This is the point of a team.

For a team to be effective, members must be given the tools and opportunities to execute their duties. Your role is to motivate, guide, and remove roadblocks. This is how credibility is earned and sustained over time.

If this micromanaging description sounds familiar to your leadership style, consider adjusting your approach. Agree with your team on a cadence for status updates and progress reviews. Establish clear communication paths for urgent matters which may arise between reviews. If you are concerned about issue which may come up between reviews, define the parameters which constitute an escalation together.

An open communication style supported by calm and steady leadership allows the team to focus on their responsibilities without feeling pressured by constant oversight. As organizational leaders, our job is to make their work easier, not harder.

There are situations where continuous monitoring of an issue, not individuals, is required to correct quickly. However, this is still different from micromanaging. Micromanagement wastes time, drains energy, and underutilizes your team's abilities. If a team member consistently requires monitoring even after proper training and ramp up, it may be necessary to reconsider their fit for the role.

There are also instances where authority alone is required for immediate compliance with short term objectives. However, those situations are typically temporary. If you are a micromanager and aspire to become an effective leader, the first step is simple: stop micromanaging immediately!

PRINCIPLE 6 Storm Readiness Checklist

Core Idea

Credibility outlasts position.

What This Looks Like

Authority can force compliance but credibility inspires commitment.

You build credibility by:

Showing up consistently and keeping your word.

Supporting your team under pressure and trusting them with responsibility.

Apply It This Week

1. Replace random check-ins with a defined cadence for updates.

2. Ask: "What support do you need?" instead of "Why isn't this done?"

3. Remember it's your job to remove roadblocks, not put them up.

Self-Check

- ✓ When something goes wrong, do I take over or support?

- ✓ Am I building dependence on me, or confidence in them?

- ✓ Would my influence remain if my title changed tomorrow?

PRINCIPLE 7: STRUCTURE ENABLES MULTITASKING

Organization is the foundation of sustainable performance.

At many instances in my career, I have led multiple active projects at once each with different milestone targets, globally dispersed teams, unique customer requirements, and emerging issues. At one point, I was managing more than twenty projects, which included a combination of new product launches and products already in series production with sporadic open issues or engineering changes arising from time to time.

At times it felt like a lot, but never overwhelming. I always managed to maintain control of each project through efficient multitasking developed over the years. The way I was able to do this can be described in one word: organization.

The ability to organize effectively is the foundation which holds everything in place to support consistent performance. However, it does not look the same for everyone. At the beginning of my career, I used Microsoft Excel sheets with all projects listed in multiple columns, with detailed information for each project captured in individual tabs.

I found myself constantly updating the information in each tab. I also observed other leaders using large project binders to organize their information, printing new documents and adding to the binders until project closure. You may get ideas from examining how others are organizing themselves.

From excel sheets, I transitioned to a digital notebook such as Microsoft's OneNote. I used it exactly like a physical notebook, with a separate notebook for each project, tabs for general project information, additional tabs for meeting minutes, and subtabs for related information, action items, and supporting documentation.

I did not replace physical notebooks for meetings because I found that it's hard to tell if you're typing into a computer responding to emails or taking meeting notes. I have seen others use a combination of excel sheets and digital notebooks, while some preferred hard copies due to long-standing habits of organization.

None of these methods are right or wrong. The key is to identify the method which works best for you, which is the one that enables you to multitask effectively without feeling overwhelmed. When you are properly organized, you reduce confusion and increase clarity on what needs to happen and when, especially when handling multiple daily requests. Only a structured system allows you to effectively juggle and manage multiple open issues simultaneously.

A proper structure also helps you remain calm when escalations arise. One of the primary reasons leaders struggle is because they feel overwhelmed by the issues at hand. With an organized structure in place, you minimize the risk of burnout and are better positioned to handle escalation items confidently and in a composed manner. When establishing your organizational structure, start simple and avoid overcomplicating it.

I have noticed that some people believe they need an elaborate organizational system that appears impressive but is intimidating to anyone unfamiliar with it. The purpose of a structured system is to serve you, not to impress others. I once showed another organizational leader how I stayed organized using OneNote, and he responded, "Wow, this looks complex and makes me dizzy!" I replied, "I would be confused and dizzy dealing with everything without it."

For your own organizational method, begin to structure it in a way that works best for you and adjust as you move along. What works for me may not work for you. However, if organization is not your strength, I suggest starting with templates available online and making the necessary adjustments so it makes the most sense to you.

There are also AI-based applications that transcribe and automatically capture meeting minutes instead of manual note-taking. I personally prefer writing things down because it helps us as humans with retention. Whatever you use, these tools should help streamline certain aspects of our job (or even personal life) with staying organized.

Another option is to seek advice from someone you know who is already organized. A colleague or friend may have a system that aligns with your thinking, and you can ask specific questions to tailor it for your needs. The key is to begin somewhere and remember the beginning is the hardest part of most things in life. Once you build and refine your structured tool over time, you will be prepared to handle whatever comes your way and multitask in a calm, composed manner.

With a structured execution method, you avoid operating purely in reactive mode. This does not mean you do not respond to issues. Instead, you respond within a structured framework regardless of what arises on any given day. It may sound easier said than done but over time you'll gain confidence because you have a structure in place.

It is possible for anyone to stay organized regardless of the complexity involved in their work. When challenging issues surface, you already understand the initial steps because your system guides you. Over time with trial and error (yes, trial and error is part of the refinement process), you will recognize patterns in your responses and standardize your approach. This means you will eventually develop a system to screen, evaluate, and deal with any issues thrown at you.

There are endless times I can think of when confronted with multiple escalations simultaneously, with all of them needing to be done yesterday. My first step was always to analyze each item and filter it through my system for managing open issues. This involved determining the true level of urgency and required completion dates. All escalations are time-sensitive, or they would not be escalations. However, it is critical to prioritize which items come first, second, and third.

Every organization operates with limited resources, meaning not all urgent problems can be addressed at once. As leaders, it is our responsibility to determine what receives attention first based on defined parameters of urgency. Those parameters vary by organization, but they are typically tied to potential impact on the customer and the company. The criteria for measuring impact are defined internally within each organization but at times are not clearly defined, meaning it is up to us as leaders to define them in order to handle escalations effectively.

Now let's think about a leader without an organizational structure for a minute. What happens when multiple issues arise simultaneously? Some leaders may perform well initially without an organized system. This may be true for some issues handled in the short term. However, over time the absence of a solid structure becomes unsustainable.

Organization is what sustains performance over the long term. It supports mental clarity and reduces stress, which in turn minimizes the risk of burnout. When you feel in control through clarity, you operate more effectively, tying back to the opening principle of this book. Everything connects to becoming a calm, composed leader.

At one point, I accepted a role working with a new and trending automotive technology. I was excited to join the team because the innovation was just entering the market. My primary responsibility was to build structure around multiple engineering teams developing the technology, which involved several layers of software development in combination with mechanical and hardware components.

After joining, I quickly realized the teams were operating within silos and lacked a unified structure. It was difficult to determine the overall project status to understand where the team was within the development phases. My first step was to meet individually with each functional team leader and ask them to explain how their function integrated into the overall system. I first needed to understand how the moving parts came together.

The next step involved bringing the teams together to establish a standardized way of working. We introduced open-issues matrixes, standardized timing plans, and a consistent reporting structure. All of these elements were introduced to standardize the process. By building a framework around the innovation teams, the overall project progress could easily be understood by the key stakeholders.

As a result, the stress levels within the core teams and management decreased significantly. The reason was straightforward: people felt more in control. The work became standardized which made it sustainable. Engineers gained clarity on which elements required higher priority because they understood where related software or mechanical components were within the development cycle at any given time.

The different engineering teams began to see the bigger picture or how the overall project was coming together. Without this perspective, it is difficult to keep functional teams aligned and working toward shared objectives. Whether you are leading a small team or an entire organization, a common set of clear deliverables is needed for solid execution. Without it, teams operate in silos at their own pace.

The concept of seeing the big picture will be discussed in detail in the next chapter under Principle 8.

PRINCIPLE 7 Storm Readiness Checklist

Core Idea

Organization protects your composure.

What This Looks Like

When everything feels urgent, structure filters noise.

Multitasking with structure creates control.

Multitasking without structure creates stress.

Apply It This Week

Make sure you can answer these in under five minutes:

1. What projects are active and what is their status?
2. What is the next milestone?
3. What is the biggest risk?

If you can't, simplify your system.

Self-Check

- ✓ Am I reacting or executing?

- ✓ Is my system of organization I've built concise and clear for me?

- ✓ If three escalations hit right now, do I know exactly what to do first?

PRINCIPLE 8: SEE THE BIG PICTURE – AND THE CONSTRAINTS

Leadership requires realism, not perfection.

There are many instances I can recall from my experience working with component suppliers who would inform us of a *force majeure*, a natural disaster, or a major issue out of their control that would cause them to stop shipping material to us under the current contract conditions. These situations usually set off alarm bells within our organization because of the corresponding scramble to find alternate suppliers to replace the broken link in the supply chain. We would then have to inform our customers who were usually the OEMs. The feedback typically sounded like this: "Find a replacement, validate (test) it, but whatever you do, don't shut us down."

When facing these circumstances, we were obviously under major constraints and tight timelines. At times we had backup suppliers, but sometimes we did not. During those instances, we needed to get creative. In some cases, the creativity involved informing the customer that we needed their help in finding a viable alternative. This was usually done through direct coordination with the customer base, investigating alternative suppliers who were on their list of approved vendors. This allowed us to speed up our own internal vendor approval processes as well.

To add to the constraints, we had to determine how much material remained in the pipeline before we ran out, in order to gauge how much time we had before being forced to shut down or preferably, switch to a fully validated product from a different supplier. If I told you everything went as smoothly, I would be lying. There were times when we had to force the switch to a different supplier without full testing under what the industry calls a *deviation*, which is essentially a special approval to proceed under certain circumstances until the full permanent approval is in place.

I do not recall any time when we shut down the OEM due to a part shortage, but I have heard of it happening. The point of my story is this: when we are working under constraints, we should view them as operating conditions rather than failures. We must adapt our operating conditions and focus on new priorities when we are forced into certain situations. We cannot focus on everything at once; this only leads to confusion and breakdowns in communication.

We must shift our focus to the specific task at hand to remain composed. When constraints arise, it is our responsibility as leaders to stay grounded by sharpening our focus on what matters most at the specific time. Whatever else we were working on needs to take a backseat or be put on the backburner. This allows us to narrow our lens and stay disciplined in addressing the issue directly.

This is part of our ability to remain agile and change gears rapidly in order to be effective. These abilities do not develop overnight but are built through experience in difficult situations like these. As I wrote earlier in the book, the best way to grow is to jump in. Over time, I have learned what works and what does not. Clear communication and avoiding promises that are out of reach are essential.

Overcommitment leads to false urgency. When you promise more than is realistically achievable, it does not matter how fast you move because you are unlikely to meet the commitment. Repeated cycles of this behavior erode morale and diminish trust within your team and organization.

Do not mistake intensity for effectiveness. We can act like we are putting out a fire by sounding alarms and promising to save everyone from a burning skyscraper. However, it is unwise to make that commitment if you do not have enough firefighters and ladders to handle the job.

I would have loved to inform our customers in every supply shortage situation that we would have a fully validated product ready before running out of material and disrupting their supply chain. In most cases, this was not reality. As effective leaders, we must manage the customer or client appropriately. We do this through upfront communication and by avoiding unrealistic promises. When constraints arise, we adapt and work as a team to find the most suitable solution.

Another important point is as leaders we sometimes allow our egos to dictate how we manage constraints. We sometimes may forget we have a network of teams and stakeholders who may provide valuable insight into our issues, regardless of complexity or technicality. If you are stuck or unsure how to handle a critical situation, ask for advice!

You may discover that someone else is better positioned to lead the issue and you may find a prime opening to delegate the task. The person or team you approach will not interpret your request as incompetence, but rather as a sign of respect and confidence in their abilities. As leaders, we need to not allow our egos to dictate our behaviors.

As a business graduate entering the automotive industry, the majority of the workforce is composed of engineers. The first thing I did at every company I've worked at was ask each engineering department for an overview of the product and their specific responsibilities. This helped me understand the details and complexities of each product I was responsible for leading through design, validation, and launch into production.

This allowed me to have a baseline understanding of the product in order to assist me in becoming familiar with the corresponding challenges in the design or manufacturing phases later. In addition, it helped me form a relationship with each of the core functional teams because I was asking for help upfront in order to understand their work.

People typically take pride in their work and it is a sign of respect to ask them to walk you through their designs and expertise. This provides a solid start to building a support network with the different functions on the team early on, especially when starting as a new leader in an organization. The benefits of speaking with each of the functions and beginning to form those relationships early are invaluable.

When your team or organization feels valued, this will show in their interactions with your customers. When the hard conversations occur, your team will have the confidence in their abilities to handle the tough situations. This will in turn distill confidence in your customer with your team's handling of the issues.

Part of seeing the big picture is not just in our specific tasks, but also realizing the way we treat our teams is reflective at our customer or client base. Maybe you've heard the expression, *take care of your employees and they will take care of your customers.* Motivated internal teams resonate the positive energy with your customers every time. I have seen this phenomenon and the opposite in many cases. It is our responsibility as leaders to ensure our teams are motivated and able to execute on their tasks in an effective manner in order to meet, manage, and exceed our customer's expectation.

PRINCIPLE 8 Storm Readiness Checklist

Core Idea

Constraints are operating conditions, not failures.

What This Looks Like

When something breaks in the supply chain (or the plan), don't chase perfection. Shift focus.

Change priorities. Communicate clearly. Avoid heroic promises.

Intensity is not effectiveness.

Apply It This Week

When a constraint hits:

1. Define the new reality.

2. Decide what moves to the backburner.

3. Communicate what you know and what you don't.

Self-Checklist

✓   Am I reacting emotionally to the constraint?

✓   Did I promise something unrealistic to ease pressure?

✓   Have I involved the right people or am I trying to solve this alone?

PRINCIPLE 9: STEP IN BEFORE YOU'RE ASKED

Proactive leadership is a choice.

If you have ever worked in a project leadership role or under a project leader, you already know who takes on tasks that fall into the "gray zone." In the automotive industry, all business entities (OEMs and tier suppliers) are required to follow a common set of quality and consistency standards established by the Automotive Industry Action Group (AIAG).

Without adherence to these standards and

the required certifications, it is not viable to supply parts to OEMs that manufacture vehicles. The presence of common standards in this industry is self-explanatory considering the safety regulations associated with automotive components. I'll get to why this is relevant in my story.

Based on these standards, tier suppliers develop a product development lifecycle model that defines who is responsible for specific tasks during each phase of design, testing, and production. I have worked for and with several automotive suppliers, often leading the project management portions of external audits for certification. There is always a "gray zone" where certain tasks are not clearly assigned to a specific function, such as falling into a specific engineering or purchasing function. These tasks are not easily identified on a RACI matrix[4].

Whenever these gray zone tasks surfaced, they consistently fell to the project or team leader. This was my experience every time, regardless of the development model, employer, or client. The team leader was expected to step in when responsibility was unclear. At times, especially when I already had a full workload, I did not always welcome this expectation. However, when ambiguity exists, the leader should step in assuming the leader has the competence or skill set to manage the task effectively.

It may appear that stepping in was always my personal decision but in reality, it was an unspoken expectation of the role. I am grateful for that expectation because over time, I realized I developed a willingness to step up in challenging situations. Even if you are not fully certain how you will resolve a problem, remember you have support. Lean on your team.

If you do not know the answer, seek guidance from someone within the organization who may have the expertise. Asking for help is not weakness. It is part of being a calm and capable leader who ensures proper understanding before moving forward.

You may recall the Allstate Insurance commercials featuring actor Dennis Haysbert ending with the line, "Are you in good hands?" The message is powerful because he projects confidence and assurance. People are naturally drawn to that sense of security. Security connects to our fundamental need for safety, one of the core human needs identified in Maslow's hierarchy of needs.

Assertiveness is closely tied to responsibility. As leaders, it is our responsibility to step forward in an assertive manner to address the challenges that arise. When we do so, we first affirm to ourselves that we are capable of handling what comes our way. We then signal to others that we believe in our own abilities and in the strength of our team. This creates a ripple effect within the organization, where motivation becomes the driving force behind execution.

I learned to become more assertive in my leadership approach as the years progressed. I remember a sitting down with a seasoned functional manager who once provided me with some constructive criticism. She indicated I needed to be more assertive in my approach with my teams in order to enhance our work. I did not take this recommendation as negative, but was grateful for her guidance in my growth.

Assertiveness does not mean forcing compliance or behaving aggressively. A leader takes control by being proactive and encouraging others to do the same. By stepping forward, you demonstrate confidence in your team's abilities and create an environment where initiative is welcomed. It is especially important for leaders to act in this way, but strong leaders also encourage others to step up before authority is formally assigned. That is where genuine leadership becomes evident, when it emerges ahead of formal designation.

Remember, leaders move things forward and don't stall the team. When something is unclear, take the initiative. If you think a certain task is better handled by someone on your team, discuss it when them directly in order to talk it through. Encouraging others to step up is part of the process of proactive leadership.

The next time a new task comes up or a gray zone action is identified, treat it as an opportunity to show proactive leadership in action. Take Action!

PRINCIPLE 9 Storm Readiness Checklist

The Core Idea

Proactive leadership is a decision.

What This Looks Like

In every organization, there are gray zones.

When no one steps up, momentum stalls.

Leaders create forward motion.

Apply It This Week

When you see ambiguity, ask:

1. Is this important?

2. Is no one owning it?

3. Can I move it forward?

If yes — step up!

Self-Checklist

- ✓ Do I wait for direction when things are unclear?

- ✓ Do I hesitate because the task isn't formally assigned?

- ✓ When ambiguity appears, do I step forward — or step back?

CONCLUSION AND FINAL THOUGHTS

When there is a storm externally, let there be calm internally. We cannot control what others do or how they react. However, our emotional state is contagious. As a leader, you set the tone for your team even when they are emotionally charged or under high stress. When you show up calm, composed, and prepared with a plan of action, stress levels begin to decrease. It is in everyone's best interest to remain steady during turbulent times.

Without a clear windshield ahead, it is difficult to navigate with both urgency and effectiveness. Sometimes that means stepping away from a situation for a few minutes and returning with a clearer perspective. Do not allow knee-jerk reactions to dictate your behavior, as those reactions are driven by emotion rather than logic.

Emotions shift quickly. Consequences tend to last much longer, especially in situations when decisions are made hastily. This does not mean operating without empathy or urgency. It means maintaining a clear mindset, defined objectives, and disciplined execution. By working this way, you become an example to your team and colleagues and contribute to their development and growth.

One practice I adopted to build a positive mindset, especially on difficult days, was simple: I would smile at myself in the mirror before work. I do not recall where the idea originated but I would look at myself in the rear-view mirror at a red light or before pulling into the parking lot and smile.

Perhaps subconsciously, this prepared me to become the person smiling back at me and reminded me of the leader I was expected to be each day. This connects to consistency, which is essential for forming healthy habits and eliminating unproductive ones. However, growth is not linear. Some days will be more challenging than others. The key is consistency until the behavior becomes automatic.

By following the guidance in the 9 principles outlined, you will be prepared to begin your journey on a solid foundation. Everything I have shared is based on years of experience in my professional career based on proven results. In addition, I have added elements of my education which have served me in the formation of my leadership principles.

For every role I have held and every client I have served, I considered my job complete not only when I delivered on expectations, but when I left the organization stronger than I found it. This is the basis for my goal with this book; to add value by sharing my knowledge and experiences for the benefit of others. If you have taken the time to read this book, I hope I have accomplished this goal with you.

ABOUT THE AUTHOR

Arben is an organizational leader and founder of Themeli Group, a consultancy focused on business development, leadership effectiveness, and international market expansions. Arben has worked domestically and abroad with multinational corporations, leading global teams in high-pressure settings. Known for his calm, structured, and integrity-driven approach, Arben emphasizes clarity, disciplined execution, and people development to drive sustainable results. He holds an MBA and is pursuing a PhD in Organizational Leadership, where his work bridges leadership theory and practice. *Leading The Storm* reflects his experience as both a practitioner and emerging scholar.

LEADERSHIP TRAINING

For information on leadership training or business consulting services, visit themeli-group.com or reach out at contact@themeli-group.com.